W9-AQV-633

Date: 01/30/12

J 599.789 KEL
Keller, Susanna.
Meet the panda /

Meet the
PANDA

Susanna Keller

PowerKiDS
press
New York

For Wendy Zeng

Published in 2010 by The Rosen Publishing Group, Inc.
29 East 21st Street, New York, NY 10010

First Edition

Editor: Amelie von Zumbusch
Book Design: Kate Laczynski
Photo Researcher: Jessica Gerweck

Photo Credits: Cover, p. 1 © www.istockphoto.com/Michael Flippo; p. 4 © www.istockphoto.com/beti gorse; pp. 6, 8, 14, 18 Shutterstock.com; p. 10 © www.agefotostock.com/JUNIORS BILDARCHIV; pp. 12, 24 stem © www.istockphoto.com/Bryan Faust; p. 16 © www.istockphoto.com/Sondra Paulson; pp. 20, 24 cub, zookeeper © www.agefotostock.com/Eric Baccega; p. 22 Getty Images/Karen Pulfer Focht; p. 24 bamboo © www.istockphoto.com/Zhu Difeng.

Library of Congress Cataloging-in-Publication Data

Keller, Susanna.
  Meet the panda / Susanna Keller. — 1st ed.
     p. cm. — (At the zoo)
  Includes index.
  ISBN 978-1-4358-9307-8 (library binding) — ISBN 978-1-4358-9726-7 (pbk.) —
ISBN 978-1-4358-9727-4 (6 pack)
  1. Giant panda—Juvenile literature. I. Title.
  QL737.C27K45 2010
  599.789—dc22
                                    2009017278

Manufactured in the United States of America

CPSIA Compliance Information: Batch #WW10PK: For Further Information contact Rosen Publishing, New York, New York at 1-800-237-9932

CONTENTS

These animals are giant pandas. Giant pandas are often just known as pandas.

Pandas come from China. However, you can see these cute animals at the zoo!

Giant pandas are big animals. Adult pandas weigh more than 200 pounds (91 kg)!

Baby pandas are called **cubs**. Young panda cubs drink their mothers' milk.

Adult pandas eat mostly **bamboo**. Bamboo is a plant with a long **stem** and many leaves.

Giant pandas eat a lot. They eat for several hours each day.

Pandas get some water from the bamboo they eat. However, they also need to drink water.

Giant pandas are good climbers. Zoos often have places for pandas to climb.

Zookeepers study giant pandas. This helps them learn how to care for pandas.

There are few wild pandas left. Studying pandas in zoos teaches us how to keep all pandas safe.

WORDS TO KNOW

bamboo

cub

stem

zookeeper

INDEX

WEB SITES

Due to the changing nature of Internet links, PowerKids Press has developed an online list of Web sites related to the subject of this book. This site is updated regularly. Please use this link to access the list:
www.powerkidslinks.com/atzoo/panda/